Dr. T's Li

Overcoming Anger in Teens and Pre-Teens:
A Parent's Guide

By Dr. Richard L. Travis

Thank You for purchasing this book.

"Overcoming Anger in Teens and Pre-Teens: A Parent's Guide"

RLT Publishing
www.rltpublishing.com
Ordering Information:
Special discounts are available on quantity purchases by corporations, associations, educators, and others. For details, contact the publisher at the above listed address.
U.S. trade bookstores and wholesalers:
Please Visit: **www.drrichardtravis.com/**

Introduction

Anger in children is often a very disturbing emotion that can have damaging, long term effects on the child if left untreated. This anger behavior often leaves parents clueless and frustrated on what the root causes of the anger are, and how to resolve it. Just like any other early childhood conditions with children, it is very crucial to spot anger immediately. Parents need to respond quickly in resolving and understanding this anger; otherwise it may lead to other chronic mental or medical conditions over time, such as depression or anxiety.

Anger in children can be a clinical issue, and is most commonly associated with children who are diagnosed with attention deficit hyperactivity disorder (ADHD), bipolar disorder and defiant disorder. Anger in children is expressed differently in preschool children, children between the ages of 5 to 12 years old, and children from 13 to 17 years of age. Since adolescent teens have developed language skills and other motor skills, they express their anger differently than children of other age groups. Their anger can be expressed more severely through engaging in actions of substance abuse, misconduct behavior, assault, verbal threats and sexual behavior.

Not all anger is "clinical" anger. This book gives parents the tools to help their child recognize their anger and express or release it appropriately. There are many ways to release anger, such as exercise, breathing, writing anger letters, stretching, and even "reframing" the cause of the anger to something more tolerable.

As a parent, you want to help your child develop coping mechanisms to deal with this anger. Parents should be well informed on childhood anger, so they can provide the best care and help to their child. Parents need to understand how anger occurs in the body physiologically, what causes and triggers anger, and how to differentiate between normal and out of control anger. This book will provide parents with all the necessary information for them to become more informed and make better decisions when dealing with anger in children.

Table of Contents

Common Misconceptions about Anger in Children

A common misconception that is associated with anger in children is that these children do not necessarily have to be misbehaving or "bad seeds." Children who suffer from anger phases can sometimes be mild mannered and well-behaved children. So what is it that causes a child to trigger their angry behavior? The reasons for that behavior will be discussed in later chapters and will give you a basic idea of how a child's brain evaluates and responds to anger.

This book will provide parents the ability to differentiate between normal anger in children and that of extreme anger shown consistently in some children. Anger in children is perceived to be a psychological problem under the DSM-IV Diagnostic Manual. It is **not,** however, considered a Disorder, such as Depression or Anxiety. If anger related behaviors are left untreated, the child slowly becomes fully consumed by negative feelings and hostile behavior which can last well into their adult lives. They begin to think it is acceptable for them to behave in this manner towards parents, friends and society. In some cases, parents let these behaviors go unnoticed until later in life, when the child has become much older. It becomes harder to cause changes in their behaviors when they are much older. Most children respond less to treatment, boundaries and rules to limit or change their behavior as they become older.

Children who have been observed with anger related behavior are often more daring in their activities. Classmates are often mesmerized at their ability to take daring chances during lunch time or after school. These behaviors could include skipping classes, engaging in pranks that harm others or participating in activities that are discouraged by authority figures. Children with anger issues normally have not been provided with proper coping mechanisms and abilities to deal with their anger. They do not have strong guidelines and structures in place to manage their anger, so they have a hard time understanding entirely the consequences of their actions.

Other types of kids with anger issues lack self-confidence and avoid activities that require social settings. Due to their anger related issues they often have a hard time concentrating and grasping academic subject matter at school. Their learning abilities are also disrupted and they feel very uncomfortable expressing academic knowledge. They often have a low tolerance for frustration which can later result in low self-esteem.

Figure 1: Child showing signs of anger

What Causes Anger in Children?

Parents need to be well informed and recognize closely what is causing these disruptive angry behaviors. There are many causes and triggers that lead to anger in children. Parents need to be on high alert and distinguish any recent drastic circumstances in the child's life that could cause them to act out. These reasons could be parental divorce, relocation, promises unmet; demands not met or failed expectations.

Angry behavior can lead children to feelings of frustrations, irritation and temper tantrums. A child can often feel frustrated with academic work at school and feel angry. When expectations are set too high, and they constantly keep failing such as in math grades, they often feel angry. Failed expectations, such as their need for parents to buy them a new toy can lead to angry behavior. Another cause for anger is irritation, such as when they are playing an activity and something keeps irritating and interrupting them during their play time. This can lead to anger related behavior. Abuse is a major cause of an anger provoking situation. When a child is abused verbally or physically, this almost always leaves scars which can often create anger boiling up inside them. Below are a few reasons why children often get angry.

Some Reasons why children can get angry:

- Death in the Family
- Parents' divorce
- Failed expectations
- Demands not met
- Promises broken
- Community violence
- Natural disaster
- Social rejection
- Too much stress
- Academic failure
- Fear
- Victim of Abuse – Verbal, Sexual, Physical or Psychological

Triggers of Anger

Understanding the trigger points is generally a very good start to understanding the pattern of your child's anger. Keep an eye out on what and when the anger is triggered in the child. Are there particular times during the day, such as after school, or certain social settings such as relatives visiting that they get angry? Most parents have often observed that their child is most likely to be angry after school. This is the time when they can release all their bottled up feelings which they have accumulated during the day. Other children are often triggered by hunger or sleep which causes them to act in an aggressive behavior. Since all children are different, there are no clear answers to what exactly the anger trigger points are. It could be school related work, a parent custody matter or a conflict with a friend. It is very important to be fully aware of what and when the anger trigger points in your child are initiated.

Watch for indicators

As a parent, it is important to be attentive about your child's eating and sleeping habits. Make sure they are getting to bed on time, and getting the adequate amount of sleep daily. If they are having trouble sleeping at night, talk to them. When kids are not getting the proper sleep, they are often more likely to throw temper tantrums and act in an aggressive manner. Below is a chart indicating the normal hours of sleep required for children for their age group.

Age Group   Required hours of sleep
3- 5 year olds   11 hours of sleep
5-12 year olds   9 hours of sleep
13-18 year olds 8.5 hours of sleep

Another action a parent should do is to quietly observe the kind of movies and TV shows your child watches. Look for similar patterns in their behavior and the characters watched on TV. Observe their favorite video games that they play, and draw conclusions if the video games have excessive violence and language. Watching age inappropriate TV shows or games can have a negative effect on the child. As a parent you should closely monitor the kind of TV shows they watch and the video games they play. If you decide that the TV shows or games are too harmful for them, then set goals with them and exclude the program from their daily schedule. Give them reasons to why the show is inappropriate for them.

Figure 2: Child watching TV

Regressive behaviors can often be types of indicators that can point to parents about their child's angry behaviors. Some children are often scared of changes such as going to day care, the first day of school, or shopping for school related material. All of these activities indicate big changes in their daily lives and indicate more responsibility. This can often cause them to show signs of regressive behaviors such as poor eating or sleeping habits. Parents can often use those signs as indicators that their child is angry. This is most commonly found in children ages 3-5, since they have not developed proper language skills yet.

Another cause of subtle anger is when children's routines have changed. They are no longer watching their favorite show on time, or not playing with their friends anymore. These changes can often trigger angry feelings as well. Parents need to keep an eye out for indicators to why their kids are getting angry. Often with young children who cannot speak appropriately, it becomes harder to determine what causes them to get angry.

How children can get angry in classrooms

There are many different types of situations, as noted by experts that cause this arousal state of anger in children. Below is a list of situations that can create angry feelings in a child in a classroom:

1. Losing control of a possession: When the child feels that their space or toys have been invaded, their state of anger arousal becomes armed.
2. Perceived verbal conflict: Such as getting teased or being mocked.
3. Physical assault: Even witnessing a physical altercation in the classroom can create an increased state of anger in the child.
4. Rejection: This happens when they are rejected by their peers, such as not playing with them, not sharing toys with them or spending time with them. This can create a state of anger.
5. Witnessing others Express Feelings of Anger with or without aggressive behavior

You need to make your child understands that there are ways to express anger without losing control. **Anger is a perfectly normal human emotion,** especially in children. It allows them to express their needs, wants and expectations. However, the problem often lies with how they express their angry feelings. Angry feelings and aggressive behavior are often two different things, and parents need to help their children be able to better differentiate between the two.

Again, it is perfectly normal for a child their age to occasionally feel angry, but sending a message that angry feelings are inappropriate can often result in damaging and harmful long term effects. Since children's brains are not fully developed, they often misinterpret meanings and information. A child who is suffering from the separation from their parent's breakup would normally have feelings of anger, anxiety and fear. It is inappropriate to tell them not to feel angry. In this example, giving them this miscued statement, can often lead children to believe that anger should be bottled up and not be shared with others.

How children can combat anger

- Develop healthy meaningful relationships with at least one parent or a close guardian
- Having Well-developed Social Skills
- Learning Problem-Solving Skills
- Learning Anger Management Skills
- Learning Self-Reflection Skills
- Developing Emotional Awareness Skills
- Seeking Optimistic Attitudes
- Learning Assertiveness Skills

Physiologically understanding why children get angry

Parents need to completely understand the biological and physiological reasons to what occurs in their child's brain when they are angry. This would provide parents the ability to better understand the child's brain system and how it responds to anger and stress. Parents can create techniques and games to calm the child's mind and body and increase their resiliency towards anger. Anger often causes the body to release adrenaline during time of stressful situations. The hypothalamus response system often uses the fight or flight mechanism to respond to the surrounding environment. This causes an increase in blood pressure, increased heart rate and results in profuse sweating.

Left and Right Hemisphere

The Left hemisphere of the brain is generally responsible for logical, language based thinking. This side of the brain basically gives us our ability to distinguish between right and wrong, what is correct and incorrect and guides us to which choices are more rationally grounded. Children often start using the left hemisphere around the age of four when they are finally capable of thinking logically.

The Right hemisphere is mostly responsible for nonlinear thinking. This side gives us the ability to understand emotions and signals all around us through our daily interactions. This is the side of the brain that is predominantly used in children. **The limbic brain** is responsible for making decisions to engage in either fight or take flight behavior. It responds to our emotions and releases stress hormones if the external situation has been deemed stressful. At around age eight, the two sides of the brain are better able to communicate with each other, hence resulting in better skills in managing anger. Children who are more heavily dominated by their right side are more controlled by their emotions. Of course, this goes for adults, too.

The Delicate Limbic System

The Limbic System might be the key area where scientists have finally figured out that is where emotional responses originate. This is the same area of the brain that causes anger in children suffering from Attention Deficit Disorder and Attention Deficit Hyperactivity Disorder. Alterations in the function in this area have often been noted to cause anger, fear and other irrational behavior. The limbic system is located in the deep interior region of the brain and often gives way to anger, anxiety, fear and other serious medical conditions such as depression. The limbic system, amygdala and the prefrontal cortex are often the regions from where we derive our critical judgments. When the correct chemical balance and adequate levels of amino acids are present in the brain, the child does not partake in negative thinking or feeling.

Amygdala

The Amygdala is the part of the brain that prepares or identifies threats as they are about to occur. It is an almond shaped structure in the brain and is often referred to as the "old watch dog." The ability of the amygdala is to warn us about the threat before the cortex can provide rational solutions. We have often observed that under stressful situations, our body is alerted much earlier, compared to our processing of rational thoughts. As soon as we observe threats, in the form of either environmental or egotistical threats, our body reacts in different ways. Our breathing rate increases, our blood pressure and heart rate increases and we get clammy hands. This is because the amygdala alerts the body prior to the prefrontal cortex's ability to make a reasonable decision. In children suffering from anxiety disorders, their amygdala is overly sensitive and perceives normal situations as threats.

When a child is angry, the brain sends out waves of chemicals called catecholamine, which increase the body's heart rate, and blood pressure rate. The breathing pattern changes and there is an increase in muscle tension. The brain now prepares to send out additional neurotransmitters and hormones such as adrenaline, which prepares the body for a fight or flight stimuli response.

Prefrontal Cortex

The prefrontal cortexes help keep the emotions in check and help us use rational judgments. As mentioned earlier, the prefrontal cortex handles judgment and awareness. Since the amygdala responds faster and is able to convince the body of a threat, the prefrontal cortex often responds after. People, who are able to stay calm under pressure, have a prefrontal cortex that is able to take control over the amygdala. It can switch off the emotions that can be felt from a stressful situation. The cortical brain plays more of a role in memory, perception awareness, thoughts and consciousness. The interactions between the prefrontal cortexes, which are part of the cortical brain, often have to respond and regulate signals from the amygdala, which is located in the limbic brain.

Genes

Genes often play a large part in determining how a child behaves or acts. Also the way children often react to stressful situations, has been role-modeled by how their parents react towards anger and violence.

Serotonin

Serotonin is an inhibitory neurotransmitter that sends electrical impulses from one neuron to another. When there are deficiencies or change in the serotonin levels, the child might become more vulnerable to anger related behavior. Serotonin levels in the child's body are often changing due to the environment around our body. If a person does not eat anything or is going through a stressful time, their serotonin level changes. This reduction in serotonin often leaves the person vulnerable to anger related behavior.

Drops in serotonin levels in the brain have often been associated with disorders such as bipolar disorder, ADHD and anxiety disorders. When there is a decrease in serotonin levels in the brain, it is often harder for the brain to communicate signals to the neurons, compared to a person with normal levels of serotonin. The communication is often made hard between the limbic system and the frontal lobe area. When the levels of serotonin are low, and communication between the brain cells and neurons have slowed down, this often makes the person highly vulnerable to hyperactive reactions and emotional complexities.

There has also been evidence of deficiency of neurotransmitters in disorders related to anger. When proper supplements of amino acids were provided, children that suffered in anger problems often reduced their anger related behavior. The lack of neurotransmitters in the brain often gives rise to the anger problems, especially in teens. Teenagers' brains are constantly undergoing change, which result in the alteration of the chemical composition of the brain.

Preschool Children (2-5 years)

It is perfectly normal for children in this age group to get angry. Since most toddlers have not developed language skills they often rely on their actions to express their anger. Hitting, Biting, Kicking, screaming and continuous crying are all signs of toddlers showing their anger. They often show signs of anger in the way they behave, interact with other children and during play activities. Biting has been noted as a sign of anger in preschool children. Preschool children often lack self-control that is shown in children in the other age groups. They have a poor sense of time, are extremely curious and often have difficulties sleeping at night. Their symptoms of anger could be indicated in their irritating actions such as constant crying or screaming. They might also crave for attention through creating a scene. Other forms of showing anger could include eating and sleeping problems.

Children 5-12 Years Old

There are many different reasons why a child may feel or express anger. Since each situation is unique, a child might feel angry due to the social and physical environment around him. If the child's parents are constantly fighting, on the verge of a breakup, or undergoing custody issues, this could lead to a very negative effect on the child, creating emotional instability. If the child is repeating the same anger behavior repeatedly in high frequency, parents need to change the structure at home, and develop rigid rules to help teach kids to control their anger. Professional intervention at a young age would also be helpful to help solve the anger issues in the child. Elementary aged children are more aggressive when they are angry, compared to preschoolers. They question adults more and are more defiant in their actions.

Children between 13- 17 years of age (teens)

Adolescent teens are far more independent than the other two age groups, and express anger similarly to those of adults. They often become irritable, defiant in their actions, act vicariously, engage in high risk behavior, suffer from low self-esteem and often distort reality. Some examples of teenage behavior that shows the presence of anger is drug abuse, shoplifting, and skipping school. Research suggests that unwarranted anger that can be quite frequent and emotionally or physically harmful to others, may be a sign of deeper emotional or psychological problems, and parents are advised to check in with their doctor.

Children expressing anger

Here are some common signs of how children express anger:

- Always arguing with adults
- Refusing to follow rules set by adults at home
- Easily getting annoyed at people's behavior and actions
- Refusing to take responsibility and often blaming others for their misbehaviors
- Being jealous and vindictive of other children
- Refusal to cooperate with teachers at school
- Refusing to follow through on their school work
- Not getting along with siblings at home
- Breaking things in the classroom or at home, and damaging other peoples properties
- Angry feelings still residing after several hours after the altercations
- Indicators from teachers at school that have raised concern over his disruptive behavior
- Being closed off, showing signs of pent up anger and resentment
- Using strong words such as hate, revenge and payback

- Not getting along with other kids at the playground
- Bullying other kids
- Verbal abuse
- Threats
- Constant screaming, shouting and yelling
- Regressive behaviors

- Child regressing in developing essential coping skills compared to other children

Physical appearance of angry behavior

- Tense body
- Clenched teeth
- Pouty face
- High intensity and tone of voice
- Restlessness and signs of regressive behavior
- Growls or loud breathing
- Angry facial expressions such as cross eyebrows
- Aggressive stance
- Easily provoked
- Squinty eyes
- Unfriendly or threatening hand gestures

Anger in Teens

Teens express their anger much differently than preschoolers or children in the age group of 5- 12 years. Their behavior is more defiant due to a need to achieve independence and a need for self-identity.

- Rude behavior and lack of respect towards adults.
- Physical fights and altercations with other students
- Rage of fits where they lose their temper and say extremely violent vindictive things
- Their motive often turns towards revenge and payback, such as breaking up with a girl or targeting the boy who cut in front of them in line at the school cafeteria.
- Mutilation, starvation or lack of social friends can often indicate signs of anger in teens
- Substance abuse is often the main way that a teen expresses their negative feelings.
- School and academic progress is usually declining and well behind the average mean

- Constantly arguing with people around them
- Verbal abuses

Figure 3: Child engaging in bullying activities on the playground

Normal vs Out of Control Anger

Differentiating between normal anger and out of control anger is really important for parents. Parents need to understand the ability to differentiate between the two. The common symptoms listed below are signs that your child's anger could be more than just normal anger.

- When your child gets angry at everything around them that stresses them. This can include rejection, perceived threat or irritation.
- When they respond to the anger by taking it too far. This can include extending the severity or the duration of the issue. When a child often talks about getting revenge or mentioning things like getting back at them.
- Since normal anger is supposed to be a temporary response system that reacts to an upsetting environment, any grievances or residing anger that has long been passed is a telling sign
- Normal regular things get them frustrated, such as waiting in line or a telephone call.

- Engaging in reckless and wild behavior that often results in property or material damage.
- Engaging in substance abuse, driving recklessly or other high risk behavior.

Figure 4: Facial expressions of anger in child

Understanding Angry Behavior

Parent's often do not know how to respond to children with anger issues. They are often embarrassed, or refuse to accept that their child has an anger problem. It is very easy to label their child's behavior as a common behavior for kids their age. But what happens when the angry behavior is gradually turned into something more severe and alarming, such as issuing threats, verbal abuse and violent outbursts? Parents need to clearly understand that this is not common behavior in children, and children do not normally behave like this at their age. Parents often make the mistakes of covering up for their child's anger issues, such as giving into their demands and buying them more toys just to make them happy. Other parents think anger is a good behavior and their child is expressing it positively. These are common fallacies that are associated with parenting an angry child. The child often lacks the ability to understand how their behavior can have a negative effect on their environment. Parents and teachers can help the child reflect on their behavior, and help provide guidance to coping with their anger.

Figure 5: Parent understanding their child's anger

Development of Skills in Children

In order to better understand how to help provide guidance to children who have anger issues, it is important to understand the gradual development of different skills in the child.

1. **Memory skills**: A child's memory often improves substantially over the course of their childhood development. This helps them remember the earlier episodes of anger related behavior. With constant memory development, children are better able to understand and cope with their anger related issues. They are able to retain past experiences as well as helpful key advice presented by parents and teachers on how to cope with anger problems. This is why older kids are able to develop anger management skills better than preschool children, who have not developed memory skills.

2. **Language skills:** Language skills develop at an individual pace differently for each child. Exposure to other children, school and even interaction at home helps Language Skills develop. Parents who create an open dialogue on issues in the child's life, help him/her to understand how to better cope with the problem. Often it is harder to explain anger related

issues to young children due to their lack of overall language skills. Once the child has developed proper language skills over time, teachers and parents expect children to understand and differentiate in their anger management abilities. There is no magic age which we can point to where the language skills will be totally sufficient to be able to process information discussed with your child. Please just be aware of what your child does understand and validate them on their understanding and new behavior.

3. **Self-regulatory skills**: Through the proper development of memory and language skills, children slowly understand their emotions and anger better. Children can learn to slowly control their anger impulses, their retaliations, frustration level, and anger arousal state, and limit their emotional outbursts. This is a developmental process, and each child has his or her own pace of development of self-regulatory skills. Parents need to be patient and consistent as the child matures through this process.

Different Intensities of Anger in Children

Anger can be felt in many different intensities and durations in children. Some anger related issues cause them to have more intensity in their anger, whereas other episodes are much calmer. Anger is often our reactions to thoughts and behaviors that were broken, disappointed or betrayed. Anger often stems from feelings of rejection, embarrassment, hurt or shame. Anger often tells the other person more about us, rather than the situation or person that made us angry. It clearly conveys to others and us to what our wants and needs are. Anger can lead to many problems. Internalizing anger can be devastating in the long run, and cause numerous problems such as heart disease, high blood pressure and depression.

The ability of the child to fight off angry feelings depends on

- Their resiliency to anger
- Age
- Ability to cope
- Stage of brain development
- Length of the stressor
- Support from family and friends

Teaching Children Anger Management Skills

Children that exhibit aggressive behavior need to be trained in regulating their emotions, so they can control their anger during stressful circumstances. Teaching them skills such as self-reflection and self-awareness can often help in creating a plan of action to control their harsh behavior. Parents can teach their children how important self-reflection is towards developing a healthy emotional development. Through asking them to engage in critical self-reflection, they would be able to explore and reflect on their inner thoughts and behaviors. This will slowly make them become more aware of their other emotions and feeling.

This will also help them identify their wants, needs and desires. It is often through self-reflection that they are able to change ourselves. All of these skills can also help create optimistic feelings in them, which help produce positive hormones in their body. These hormones help increase their resiliency towards anger and help improve their positive thoughts. <u>Optimistic feelings and behaviors are important techniques that can help counterattack the angry feelings in your child's mind.</u>

In a modern day society, where it appears that hostility and aggression is all around us, it often gives mixed signals to our youth that the world is hostile and out of control. This often creates feelings of fear in the child and gives way to anger. When a child observes hostile and aggressive behavior around them in the news, community or family, they often create feelings of anger in themselves as well. Parents and kids both need to realize to realize that anger is part of our daily lives and is a natural human emotion depicted in any age group. It falls into a category with our other emotions such as love, guilt, fear and sadness, and helps us define ourselves as humans. The range of emotions that humans can express is what makes humans unique.

Self- Reflection

Metacognition refers to our ability to self-reflect, avoid denial and reach rational effective plans to change the course of our behavior. One way to engage in this process is to learn breathing techniques, which can often have impact on both the child and the parent. As the parent, they have to be very self-reflective and critical of their own behavior as well. The way parents behave or carry themselves around children unknowingly can also have a great impact on how the child views the world. If the tone of your voice or body language depicts aggressive behavior, your child might believe that it is normal to act in this manner.

This is because the prefrontal cortex side of their brain which is responsible for rational thoughts and interpreting signals around them is not fully developed. Perception can often be miscued in the child's mind.

Mindful breathing techniques can often help us increase our resiliency towards stressful situations and help calm our stress response system. Adults and children often breathe using the upper portions of their lungs which result in shallow breathing. The capability to fill our lungs completely with air allows us to relax our body and calm our minds.

An angry outburst in the family can have positive changes in the family as well. After the anger ordeal, discuss the situation as a family and reflect back on what the problem was once everyone has cooled off. This can help in creating a set plan in action to avoid the problem if it occurs again. It helps the parent and the children develop and cope with different skills to deal with anger management as a family. This can help children develop excellent coping mechanism to deal with anger. After an anger ordeal has occurred, it is important for the family to reflect back on the anger session and reflect on what they have learned. This will improve self-awareness of emotions in the child, problem solving skills, assertiveness skills and healthy thinking skills which are all crucial to developing anger management skills. This will help them develop key problem solving skills which can be greatly beneficial in the long run.

It often teaches them to bring a closure to the anger related incident and take lessons learned from it. This helps avoid any bottled up feelings one might carry. Another skill that is learned is assertiveness skills. This means that the child learns the ability to convey their needs, wants and expectations in a calm and positive way. They realize the needs of others and do not consider their needs above everyone else.

Another skill the child can develop through self-reflection is the ability to look at situations realistically. If they have a friend that always cancels out, rather than immediately jumping to conclusions and being angry. They can use their healthy positive thinking and rationally realize that their friend does not usually back out of a plan and may have been busy during that week. This gives the child the ability to properly rationalize and assess situations realistically.

Playing games such as describing certain strange objects can help the child express his feelings and thoughts with words more creatively. Take your child to the park and find a quiet corner. Find small objects or scenery nearby and tell them to describe it to you, while you keep your eyes closed. Through using words to describe that object they will be able to communicate more effectively and clearly.

Figure 6: Parent playing activities that help develop anger management skills

Deep Breathing

Teach children the ability to breathe using the lower parts of their lungs. Deep breathing has been labeled as the secret solution to some of the most common mood swings. Explain to your children how deep breathing can often calm the mind and body. Deep breathing can help calm the amygdala which causes the responses of our stress hormones. You can explain to your child that amygdala is like the old security watch dog who stands at the front of the gate. Whenever the amygdala perceives threatening behavior, it starts alerting and sending signals and stress hormones all throughout our body.

The art of mindful breathing would allow them to calm the amygdala, which is in some cases is overly sensitive to the external surroundings around us. Teach your children to incorporate five minutes of deep breathing into their lives every day. Deep breathing also helps by releasing good hormones such as dopamine and serotonin. Deep breathing allows us to strengthen our self-reflective abilities, self-awareness and increase emotional control, which can result in better controlling of our anger. Tell them to place their hand on their bellies as they are taking in deep breaths, and exhale out slowly. Feel the diaphragm fill with air as they inhale.

Playing games that make them become aware of their pulse rate and breathing patterns are also very helpful. Tell your child to sit down in a quiet room and place their two fingers on their wrists, locating their pulse, and gently hold their fingers there. Then tell them to count the number of the pulse rate that occurs in one minute.

After they have counted the total number of times for the pulse rate, tell them to go run outside for 3-4 minutes. They can do jumping jacks, run in the backyard or any other kind of small physical activity. When they are done, tell them to return to their quiet corner and place their fingers over their wrist again, and count the number of the pulse rate that occurs for one minute.

Showing them the difference in the changes of the pulse rates allows them to understand the changes in their body and heart rate. They can gradually use this technique to figure out if they are angry or not. Being in tune and understanding your pulse rate can be important for children to monitor their angry behavior. Teach them what normal expected pulse rates are, and what extreme pulse rates can be.

Emotional Awareness

Parents can help children become more aware of their feelings and emotions. If something is gently bothering them, or a stressful situation is gradually about to take place, you can detect the predictable event to likely occur and remove them from it. For example, Johnny decided to play with Mark one day instead of your child. As a parent you can detect that this could slowly upset and cause angry feelings inside your child. You can teach them the ability to detect stressful situations and remove themselves from circumstances that hurt them. The more they are able to better understand their own feelings and emotions, the more likely they are to keep them in check.

Teach them how to control their emotions and stay relaxed. Deep breathing techniques can often come in handy at this stage. It is important not to reach the boiling point, and try to calm the body and mind. Try to bring the body temperature back to normal in order to control your anger. This will eventually help in regulating your state of anger arousal. Help develop small changes in your child's thinking patterns. This way they can manage emotions better and understand reality clearly. Teach them how to use empathy to understand how other people might deal with this problem, or how it would feel like to walk in their shoes.

You can play games with them that can raise their emotional awareness and be better able to identify people's emotions and feelings. The next time you take your child driving around in the car, you can play a game with them and ask them to generally recognize how that person walking outside is feeling. The child can use their body language, facial expressions and style of behavior to access what mood they are in. This will help improve the child's ability to recognize emotions and feelings in other people.

You can even use them in an example; put a couple of different CD's on and ask the child to listen to each of the songs. While they are listening to the different tone, voices and intensity of song ask them to describe what they feel during the different songs. Does the song make them feel like getting up and dancing, getting sad or maybe makes them happy. This will make them more in tune with their feelings and emotions.

Figure 7: Playing games that teach them how to be more emotionally aware

Helping Your Child Release Anger

-----*Mirror work.*

Take some time every day to look into the mirror and tell yourself that you love and accept yourself just as you are. Do it privately, so you can do it **out loud**. The more you say it, the more powerful and true the words will feel. This may seem silly at first, but the purpose is to purely interrupt the other belief that you have which is the opposite--"I don't love or accept myself as I am. I would have to be different to love and accept myself."

If the exercise seems too basic, it really is just a step towards changing the negative "hardwired" beliefs that have limited you, and perhaps moved you towards that validation seeking behavior. It is a step. It is a step that needs to be taken and will have a major effect on your self-esteem. Another statement that anyone can say while looking into a mirror is: "I am not the anger, the anger is not me." "I am Richard, and I am not the anger." Words such as these help distance the child or adult from the anger, also detaching from it.

-----*Journaling*

There are many books written about how to journal and why it is important. For the compulsive person, or addictive person, or an angry person it does really provide an insight into the thoughts and feelings experienced daily of the person writing the journal. Typically, it is good to spend 10 to 20 minutes everyday, while in therapy, writing in your journal. There don't have to be a great many rules as to what you write.

You could write a gratitude list once a week, or even daily. You could write your fears or worries and give them to God. You could write letters to people who have hurt you or to whom you hold resentments. You could just write what you are feeling today. No matter what you write, it is private and personal and should not be shared with anyone.

Most people feel that keeping a journal helps them peel off layers of old hurt and anger. You may even be angry at yourself for choices that you have made. Write an Anger Letter to yourself. Make a list of people to write Anger Letters to. Use your private journal to write these letters, and never let anyone see them. You may even choose to burn the anger letters after you have written them. After you have completed an Anger Letter, visualize the anger that was within you leaves you, and replace it with Peace and Calm.

-----*Meditation*

Meditation has been used for eons to bring a level of calm and inner peace to generations of people. While often used as a form of mental discipline, it can help those with anxiety by focusing on the here-and-now and give something to focus on. There are dozens of types of meditation but some of those which can have the most positive effect on self-esteem are below. Again, these are just a few of many available.

- **Zen Meditation –** This type of meditation sometimes uses visualizations and, as shown in the photograph above, integrates your posture and your breathing. Its goal is to raise the level of your self-awareness and force the negative thoughts out and away from you. Concentrate deliberately on your breathing. Slow it down and take deep breaths. This causes the brain to enter a tranquil state and calm you.

- **Meditation With a Mantra –** This form of meditation uses the repetition of a word or phrase many times in order to achieve a state of peace and the ability to view your negative thoughts "from afar" so that you can focus on observing them rather than living them.

- **Mindfulness Meditation** – Having its roots in Buddhism, this type of meditation focuses on you becoming *more* focused on your feelings and thoughts so that you *can* live in the here-and-now. Essentially, it's a form of facing your anxiety head on and trying to conquer it.

Those who wish to try meditation as a form of dealing with their self-concept can learn through the many readily-available web sites, CDs, books, articles and yoga studios that teach the different methods. Resources are below:

Meditation Oasis Website for Information and Select Meditations: http://www.meditationoasis.com

Many Guided Imagery Scripts and Articles—Just type in "Guided Imagery" in the Search Box: www.Ehow.com

Article: Guided Imagery

http://www.Livestrong.com/article/164001-visualization-guided-imagery/

YouTube Guided Imagery Selection:

http://www.bing.com/videos/search?q=guided+imagery+youtube&qpvt=guided+imagery+youtube&FORM=VDRE

----Creative Visualization

Many people believe there is great power in creative visualization. This is the process where someone used a CD, or DVD to guide them through an imaginative exercise. The purpose in this case would be to close your eyes and visualize yourself happy, competent, likeable, and participating with others.

There are many quality CDs and DVDs available to guide someone through a Creative Visualization. The key is to find a voice that you like and an imagery that fits your needs. When you practice visualizing the anger leaving you and all of the causes of it too, don't forget to replace the anger with peace and happiness in the places in your mind and body formerly harboring the anger.

Disorders

In some cases, anger is part of the problem of a bigger medical condition such as a mental or mood disorders. In the case of children suffering from ADHD, or Oppositional-Defiant Disorder, anger is one of the common symptoms. When children suffer from these disorders, they often depict angry hostile feelings toward their environment. It is best to talk to your doctor, when the child shows continuing feelings or behaviors related to anger.

If the anger related behavior is more frequent, then they are more likely a part of a serious anger issue such as disorders.

- Anger disorder
- Oppositional Defiance Disorder
- Bipolar Disorder
- Attention Deficit Hyperactive Disorder
- Conduct Disorder
- Depression
- Anger Addiction

Bipolar disorder

Some children cannot control their anger due to serious mental disorders which lead to anger issues. Children suffering from bipolar disorder undergo severe mood swings, immature and irrational behavior. Children with bipolar disorder often go untreated until 11 or 12 years old.

This causes their disorder to escalade to extreme forms of mood swings and can lead to other problems such as depression. If it is left untreated further, it often leads to suicidal thoughts and can often make life unbearable for them. Children who suffer from mental disorders such as Bipolar disorder need to seek professional help immediately.

Before helping a child manages their anger, you as the parent need to understand anger. From the early studies of Lewis and Michalson, they detected that anger in children generally had three components; the emotional state of anger, expression of anger and understanding of anger. The emotional state of anger is the moment when the child feels like they have been turned down or perceive frustration and rejection. It is the arousal state of feeling angry when their needs are not complied to.

Attention Deficit Hyperactivity Disorder

Attention Deficit Hyperactivity Disorder is one of the most recognizable disorder commonly found in children. 60% of children that suffer from ADHD continue this developmental problem to their later years of adulthood. Currently 8 million adults suffer from ADHD. Approximately 3 to 10 % of children suffer from ADHD in the United States and approximately 60 % of those children will carry ADHD into their adult lives. ADHD is more commonly found in boys than girls; however girls often suffer from this disorder as well. One of the common symptoms for ADHD children is the difficulty in controlling their anger. Children with ADHD tend to express their negative feelings and anger much strongly than normal children. This makes tasks such as homework, learning assignments, making friends and being in social environments all the more difficult for them. Children that suffer from ADHD often have poor academic performances and are more likely to fail or drop out of school. This often shows up later in their work life as well, as they change jobs much more frequently and have lower levels of satisfaction with their jobs. Their relationships are also likely to suffer and result in higher rates of separations with their spouses.

Anger disorder

More than 15 million American currently suffer from anger disorders in the United States. Children that exhibit in aggressive, violent and destructive behaviors have unresolved issues of anger in them. They have not been provided the proper coping abilities to better manage their anger. They are more prone to repressing their anger and have sudden angry outburst. Their behaviors and social patterns are often unpredictable which make it hard for them to have friends or be in social environments. They are unreliable in work environments as well and can cause stress to their coworkers. They slowly harbor angry feelings of resentment, bitterness and rage. It creates a higher likelihood of substance abuse and destructive rage. The underlying cause of their anger must be recognized and treated properly. Their destructive anger could be nurtured towards a constructive or creative outlook. They usually suffer from impulsive control issues which makes it harder for them to resist activities that have high levels of risk associated behavior such as violence or property destruction.

Figure 8: Parent frustrated with child that suffers from anger disorder

Things your children should not do when they get angry

There are a couple things you should encourage your child to never do when they get angry. Never bottle or repress up those angry feelings. Listen to them and allow them to release their anger in a positive and calm manner. Just by you engaging with them and listening to them, allows them an outlet to relieve their anger. This is very crucial because if the parent does not provide an outlet for the child, the child can continue to bottle up the feelings. This can be harmful as it creates a toxic environment in their body. It often leads to feelings of resentment and hatred in you. When a child reacts quickly to anger or gets defensive extremely quick, this is also a behavior that should be discouraged by parents. Tell them never to harm themselves or others verbally or physically during their state of anger, since it can lead to consequences such as timeouts and suspension. Lastly parents should talk to their child about impulsive behavior. Anger often causes us to lose our rational thinking and causes us to act out on impulse. We often regret that action later and can cause damages in our personal and social lives. It is very important to explain this to kids clearly and explain to them the negative effects of aggression.

Tips for parents

Children often act out when their angry and can often leave the parents in a state of shock and confusion. They often do not know what is bothering their child and what the root cause of anger is. Here are a few suggestions that parents should do to help their children manage and better control their anger. Parents can help their children develop several of these abilities through learning about practical tips, helping them develop coping skills, advice, anger management games and healthy anger related exercises.

One of the common mistakes that parents do in this state of confusion is that they often give in to their child's demands. They think that this is the best way to calm them and make them happy. Make sure to not give in to your child's demands as this will reaffirm to them that angry outburst leads to positive results. Talk to the child in a nice calm manner, do not lecture them. After their angry outburst has mellowed down, praise your child for how they have controlled their anger. Talk to them about their behavior and how proud you are of them.

Parents can

- Show warmth and affection to their child
- Don't lecture or punish them
- Have clear but reasonable expectations of them
- Do not be controlling or have rigid structures
- Talk to them in soft tone voice
- Spend more time with them

- Listen to them
- Give them hugs, kisses and emotional support
- Teach them anger management strategies
- Praise them regularly especially when they show signs of controlling anger
- Acknowledge their angry feelings
- Be proactive rather than being reactive
- Asking open ended questions on ways to deal with their angry feelings
- Teach them deep breathing exercises
- Ways to avoid stress
- Try to reason with them when they are calm, do not reason with them when they are enraged.

Figure 9: Parent spending time with their child

Reacting or Responding

Reactive behaviors are usually punishment behaviors that parents present to their kids after they have behaved aggressively. These reactive measures are usually in the form of timeouts, grounding or even in some cases spanking. They are quick, temporary forms of disciplinary action that have been noted to give the wrong message to kids. The message that children often derive from this is that it is okay for parents to hit a child when they have behaved badly. Impulsive quick reactions by parents create negative emotions in the child and does more harm than good. The best action for parents dealing with a child who is angry is to respond appropriately. Parents want to be able to help their child develop their coping abilities to better avoid angry behavior in the long run. It will help them avoid social, marital or work related problems that occur in their future adult lives due to anger related problems.

Figure 10: Reactive Measures shown by Parents

Parents need to get involved and confront their child

One of the most important things that parents can do is intervene early in the child's life. Do not think that the anger is normal for their age and let it escalade into regular angry behavior. You will have to tactfully engage them without bringing up their bad behavior. Observe what the child likes, if they like physical contact such as hugs; give more of it to them. If they have a favorite treat, give it to them. Slowly, once you build that regular communication with them, you can open up to them and discuss their irrational behavior.

Provide choices

Another common technique used with kids dealing with anger issues is to allow them options and choices. Do not always have a firm schedule in place for them to follow. Often kids with inflexible routines feel trapped and helpless and this could lead to harboring deep anger issues. Allow them to have control over their choices in games, movies and play activity. Design a method, where you can present them two or three safe options to choose from. This will create an immense change in their behavior and feeling towards their environment.

Spend time with them

Common activities shared between the two of you daily could also help you reach out to him. Develop a certain activity daily that you and your child can share. This can include TV time, reading books together or playing a small game of snakes and ladders every night. The point is to share an activity together. Also another common technique that has been tested is to discuss with them fictional story characters that have shown similar anger problems. Using another character from fictional stories can often help kids visualize and relate to the character from a fantasy world. Show them how this character behaved badly and the consequences he suffered from his anger, such as his loss of super powers. This can also open the doorway for immediate feedback and discussion on the topic of how to control and manage anger. Your child will present his feedback to what the character could have done differently to avoid the situation. Parents engaging in activities that include both the children and the parent can improve his level of communication, emotional awareness and self-esteem.

Children who are often neglected at home find it hard to express themselves and develop improper anger management skills. They are usually left with a weak anger management system in place as they deal with life's stressful situations all throughout adulthood. By opening a communication channel between the two of you, you are immediately helping them build trust and feel more relaxed.

Parent's Behavior

Parents have to pay attention to themselves and their own behavior. This would require a self-assessment of their own behaviors and actions towards their child. Parents can unknowingly raise the tone of their voice, give a stern look or depict aggressive language when talking to their child. Some parents often believe that the best way of getting through their children is to make them afraid. Parents need to show their child unconditional love and teach them that they will be loved no matter what.

Sleep issues

Since children are often too nervous to sleep at night, due to their anger related issues. Deep breathing can help them sleep better at night. If a child is angry, they are more likely stressed out, which causes the inability to sleep at night. This in turn causes them to be more moody and irritable the next day. It is a cycle that just repeats itself just because the body cannot get enough rest.

Timeouts

The long duration of timeouts is generally discouraged when dealing with children with anger problems. Usually timeouts have a negative connotation to them as a disciplinary or a punishment measure. Although, this is correct, timeout in this case can serve an alternative and positive purpose altogether. It can teach the child to cope with their anger problems in a healthy and calm manner. Timeouts can be a great way for a child to remove themselves from that hostile environment and bring their body response system back to normal. A change of scenario is critical during this process, as it can help calm the child down. It is important for them to completely remove themselves of the environment that makes them angry.

Parents should not engage with them about the angry situation while they are in time outs. This will only make matters worse and revive the aggressive situation. Let them cool down and spend some time by themselves to relax their body and clear their mind. When dealing with children who have blown up during a stressful situation, ask them what they could have done differently. If they could have expressed their feelings differently, things may have been a little less destructive.

Figure 11: Parents directing child to timeout

The techniques that worked earlier, such as timeouts, are often ineffective with adolescent teens. Time outs have been known to lose their effectiveness at the ages of twelve and thirteen. The adolescent brain often undergoes changes in the frontal lobe and other areas. Most of the anger that arises in adolescent teens stems from the fact that they are no longer kids, but yet not fully developed as an adult. They are often psychologically shifting towards more independence and exploring their own sense of identity. This often clashes with the parent's natural instinct to continue to protect their kids and are still treating them as young kids. Time outs can be a good short term solution for preschoolers and children that fall in the age group of 5-12 years old. Timeouts have to be modified though. For teens, have them engage in a self-assessment of their behavior, as they may need to cool off or take their mind off the angry situations. Using timeouts effectively for these reasons can prove very helpful for the child, and can utilize the effects of timeout completely rather than just as a disciplinary, reactive measure.

Temper tantrums

Young children often go through ranges of temper tantrums when they are upset or angry. As mentioned before, anger comes in different ranges of intensities and durations. The higher intensities cause the child to burst out and throw raging temper tantrums. The common symptoms of a temper tantrum is the child crying, yelling, screaming and shouting for longer periods of time than normal. It is their way of either getting attention or letting out their angry feelings. It is important to understand and assess your child's anger, such as when they specifically get angry and it may be related to being hungry or tired.

Children are said to grow out of severe unwanted temper tantrums around the age of four. This is when their brain is continually developing, and they become more aware of their emotions and feelings. However anger in children is often a major cause of concern to parents when the child is engaging in activities that are not normal for their age. This includes violent behavior, excessive emotional outburst and emotion instability. When a child is throwing temper tantrums, do not punish them for it and do not reward them either. Make sure to keep them in a safe place and remove any harmful or sharp objects around them. Since they are extremely hyper during the middle of a temper tantrum, it is easy to cause hurt to self or others. Parents have to stay in control and regain their authoritative position to bring calmness back in the environment. Do not yell, argue or punish them as this may only make future temper tantrums worse. A temper tantrum is most commonly found in children around the age of 2. This is usually why they call the second year the "terrible twos." This is because they can feel and sense more than what they can express, due to their inability to speak.

Stress

Children go through many stressful situations such as first day of school, making new friends, facing social rejection, coping with academic studies and sleeping in the dark. Many adolescent teens go through phases of independence where they search their sense of identity. We all go through life's stressful situations and turbulence. Dealing with life is like riding a wild roller coaster of emotions. There are high, uplifting moments which cause us to celebrate and be happy, and there are life's down moments where we often feel we've hit rock bottom. Children, just like adults will go through various stages of life, where they will meet stressful situations. An unhealthy response mechanism to stress can cause poor coping abilities and lead to outbursts of angry issues.

Stress can result in:

- Stomach aches
- Nervousness
- Trouble sleeping
- Anger

Teens' Perception of Reality

Teens are often the most difficult to deal with due to their level of defiant behavior and their severity of anger expressed. Teens often perceive reality different from adults. There is always a constant power struggle where the teen wants to attain personal independence and the parents hang on to their natural protective nature. There are four types of perceiving thoughts that occur in young teens.

- **Reality distortions**: This is when teens assume things in their mind and jump to conclusions. Often listening to half of the conversation and making up their thoughts prior to the completion of the conversation. The negative thoughts in their head often give way to underlying frustration and dysfunctional anger.
- **Discomfort intolerance**: When teens perceive a threat to their image or their well-being, they often become highly alert and vigilant.
- **Expectations that become demands**: This is persistent in teens when they turn expectations into demands. Anything that is not met accordingly by them puts them in a state of anger arousal. These kinds of expectations often give way to demanding people to act or behave a certain way. If people don't act accordingly to what they prefer, they often get angry.
- **Name calling**: To make themselves feel better, teens often call some other person names, due to them

not meeting their expectations or demands. For example, if Johnny does not like how Mike behaves in public, he will often criticize Mike about that point. The constant criticizing of Mike is so he can modify his behaviors and meet Johnny's demands.

Tips to Manage Anger in Teens

These tips have been very helpful in teens to help them manage their anger.

- **Exercise**: Going for a walk, run or working out can often release pent up anger and produce more stress reducing chemicals that relax the body. It is a great way to control your anger problem
- **Music**: Music can often help us change our feelings, mood and body. The soothing vibrations and effects have been evident in uplifting the person's mood, releasing tension and other stress related behavior
- **Sports**: Engaging in sports related activity can once again alleviate the body from any mental stress and reduce feeling depressed or sad
- **Deep breathing:** The art of deep breathing or meditation can often help our body feel relaxed and calm. It is often a common practice for adults to use meditating and deep breathing practices to release their anger. Teach teens the art of deep breathing effectively and it will drastically help them.

- **Activities/ hobbies**: Indulge in your favorite pass-time activity: If they have a preference for reading comic books, or watching their favorite movie, it is highly recommended that they participate in that to distract their mind from the tension.

Cognitive Behavior Therapy

Cognitive Behavioral therapy is often the most prescribed therapy by doctors when dealing with anger management. The therapy consists of three important parts which includes changing the cognitive structure, developing behavioral skills and physiological relaxation techniques. As discussed earlier, people with anger issues often have low level of frustration, distorted realities or assumptions, hypersensitivity to threats and overgeneralizations. These can impact their thoughts, behaviors and feelings and physiologically cause alterations in the body.

The patient is required to systematically list a variety of options and alternatives that they can chose from. The first step is to generalize what is wrong with their thinking patterns and explore the errors in them. The client is asked to assess whether the anger is justified or over generalized. Patients are then taught relaxing techniques to help negate the negative feelings after they have discovered their cognitive or thinking errors. This can include relaxation of different muscles and stress stimulators located in the body. The doctor also puts them in anger stimulated activities to help guide them on how to control their anger. The client by this stage has developed changed cognitive strategies, anger awareness and relaxation techniques. The last step includes behavior building skills in them which include several phases. They are taught techniques such as having a calm tone of voice, appropriate body language, and non-threatening eye contact. The environment may be manipulated to cause simulated stress in them which can lead to anger. This can include hunger, or even tiredness to engage in anger provoking situations. After the client has been trained in anger coping activities and behavioral techniques, the anger provoking situation is removed. These interactions can often calm their mind and provide them with behavioral skills during their state of anger. All these behaviors and techniques are developed through modified role play sessions.

A Final Thought to Parents

Parents often need to stay calm during their child's angry emotions. Although the child shows signs of angry behavior, the longevity of their behavior depends on their parents and the coping skills they provide for their child. Parents should never lose their calm and control when dealing with children who are angry. They should always listen to them, console them and try to understand their root causes and triggers of anger. Slowly engage in activities with them to improve their sense of feeling and expressing themselves without using angry behavior. The more time parents spend nurturing these abilities in their child, the more likely the chances that the child develops successful anger management skills to combat throughout their adult life. After all, isn't that the role of parents instead of grounding them again and again?

Figure 12: Children should always feel loved even if they show signs of angry behavior

A Technique from the Author

Hurt turns to resentment, resentment turns to anger, and anger turns to rage!!!

This is a concept which I present to everyone to help interrupt isolated anger incidents, whether as a teen, pre-teen or adult. If someone is angry and willing to sit and talk about it, then ask one question; "What are you really feeling underneath that anger?" Promote a discussion about any feelings that might come up. Ultimately, my goal is to get the teen to discover that there is almost always a "hurt" that is the precursor to the anger. If we can discover the hurt, and then express the hurt, in an appropriate way, we can interrupt the escalation of the emotions that often end up in anger.

So what is an appropriate way to express the hurt? Having a friend or family member who we feel safe enough to confide in about an incident where our feelings were just hurt is very helpful. This usually is all most children and adults need, to interrupt the escalation of feelings.

If you notice that your teen is especially sarcastic lately, but willing to sit and talk, then again ask the question; "What are you feeling underneath all of that sarcasm?" Promote a discussion of feelings. Again, I believe that HURT is the culprit and needs to be identified, expressed and released. Try It! You need to make the teen feel very SAFE to talk about these feelings.

Most people, teens included, who are walking around very, very angry would need more than this technique to release hurt and then desensitize the anger. Most people need to work through the anger, expressing it verbally, physically or on paper. But, I truly believe that if we can express HURT when it comes up, we can do a great service to ourselves in interrupting the escalation of feelings to Resentment, Anger and Rage.

Self-Esteem Enhancers.......

These Self-Esteem Enhancers are actually "affirmations" which are deeply rooted in history....

The theory is that we have become programmed by parents, siblings, society, television, the internet, the media, etc., and this programming has led to our attitudes about ourselves and others. This programming is very often negative, leaving us with a negative self-image.

By taking a positive statement, such as a Self-Esteem Enhancer attached, and repeating it for 7 to 21 days, we begin to change that programming. <u>The more we repeat the statement, and the more feeling behind it, the stronger and quicker the results.</u>

Thinking the statement you pick for 10 times each day is <u>okay,</u> saying it out loud 10 times is <u>good,</u> and saying out loud it and writing it 10 times daily <u>is excellent</u>. One way to begin reprogramming yourself is to mentally repeat the Self-Esteem Enhancer as many times as you can during the day when you have a few free minutes.

****

<u>Directions</u>: Say the Self-Esteem Enhancer which you choose, 10 times in the morning just after rising, and 10 times in the evening just before bed for 7 to 21 days. Say it out loud if at all possible. Looking in a mirror while saying it, gives extra power to the activity. Also, the more times you say it, the quicker and more powerful the results. Concentrate on one Self-Esteem Enhancer at a time for best results. Also, don't share your Self-Esteem Enhancer with anyone else, as you don't want any chance of

someone's negative thoughts or comments weakening your efforts to make a positive change in yourself. Good Luck and Bon Voyage on your journey to loving yourself more completely..........

My life is a series of choices and I choose only positive and loving interactions with others.

———

For the next 24 hours I will attract only positive, loving situations.

———

The negativity of others bounces off me and I remain centered, focused and clear.

———

I love my mind and my body.

———

I leave my negative self-image behind me and see only a positive love-filled me.

———

Others are attracted to my loving, peaceful nature. I radiate contentment.

———

My loving thoughts chase away all fear.

———

I easily release all anger in an appropriate way.

———

I release and let go of any need to feel guilty.

I radiate peace and contentment.

I forgive myself for living in shame and guilt and easily release the need to feel these limiting feelings.

I release those who I feel have limited or victimized me, by understanding, loving and forgiving them.

I choose peace, love and joy as my companions today.

The child within me plays in the moment and experiences freedom and joy.

This is my day to feel peace, love and harmony in all that I say and do.

I deserve to experience peace, love and harmony.

I am worthy of love.

I am honest, open and loving in all that I say and do.

I believe in ME!

I like myself.

I am loveable.

I feel good about myself.

I have faith in myself.

I love myself.

I am confident.

I now accept myself and others exactly as we are.

Every day I grow to love myself more and more.

I believe in myself.

My thoughts are positive and loving, and I am always attracting this in others.

I am beautiful and loveable and have a great deal to share with others.

Every day, in every way, I grow more and more positive, calmer and at peace with myself.

I am a positive influence in all situations I encounter.

I am lovable and capable.

The child within me finds healthy ways of play and self-expression.

I believe in ME!

I allow myself to relax and be at peace.

I am a positive influence in all situations I encounter.

I am positive and loving.

I am source of great joy and creativity.

Every day I grow to know and accept myself more and more.

I am beautiful and lovable and have a great deal to share with others.

Every day, in every way, I am getting better and better.

Improving Self-Image Script (A Guided Imagery Exercise)

"Find a comfortable place to relax, and make sure your arms and legs are uncrossed... become aware of your breath...and let's begin by taking three slow, deep breaths... Now close your eyes... and let the muscles in and around your eyes relax, and let your eyelids relax... and continue to let your eyelids relax...Let them relax so much that they won't work, even if you tried... Now let that relaxation flow up to your forehead and scalp.

Now let that relaxation flow out to your cheeks, and mouth, and chin... Let that relaxation flow down from your eyes, over your torso, and all the way down to your feet. Just allow the relaxation to take over your entire body now as you let go... just let go...

I'm going to count down from 10 to 1, and with each descending number, feel a wave of relaxation flowing over you, and flowing through you, relaxing every muscle, every tissue, every cell.

10... 9, feel the waves of relaxation...

8... 7, feel the relaxation flowing through you...

6... 5, more and more relaxed...

4... 3...letting go of today and relaxing more and more...

2... 1...very relaxed and comfortable...

Now scan your body and search for any remaining pockets of tension and on your next few exhales, exhale that tension that is stored in any muscles or tissues, exhale it right out... more and more relaxed with every gentle breath you take... more and more relaxed with every gentle breath you take... Now keeping your eyes closed, become aware of an image screen in front of your forehead, and on this image screen is your private showing of a wonderful healing image.

The first image I'd like you to visualize is that of a very secret or special place that only you can go to. It may be a forest or a pond, a beach or a field, a special room or a mountain. Whatever it is you have visualized, become aware of the colors in your special place, become aware of the three dimensions all around you, as you are now in your special place; relaxing, more and more with every breath...

This special place is a place for you to do some inner work, some healing...While relaxing in your special place I'm going to say statements to you, and as I say each statement, affirm it to be true by saying it to yourself, in your mind. Know these things to be true! There is no reason to think about these statements, so just let your conscious mind drift off. Just feel them, feel them opening up every cell of your being, cleansing and healing.

"Every day in every way, I am getting better and better..."

"Every day in every way, I am getting better and better..."

"Every day I am growing to know and accept myself more and more..."

"Every day I am growing to know and accept myself more and more..."

"Every day I am growing to love myself more and more..."

"Every day I am growing to love myself more and more..."

"Love is the opposite of fear. Where there's fear there is no love..."

"Love is the opposite of fear. Where there's fear there is no love..."

"My loving thoughts chase away all fear..."

"My loving thoughts chase away all fear..."

Know that every cell of your body has intelligence and can open up to relax to healing and cleansing... and every gentle breath takes you deeper and deeper relaxed. Every gentle breath takes you deeper and deeper relaxed.

Become aware now on your image screen in front of your head the image of a beautiful mansion-- a mansion of your design. It can be one that you've seen before, or just one you're creating right now... Slowly approach the mansion from the front, and enter the front door... and step into the foyer or the entrance of this wondrous mansion, and walk around and see the beautiful furniture, the paintings, the decorations...

Become aware of a beautiful staircase leading up to the second floor... Now proceed up this staircase and know in your heart that wonderful things await you at the top of these stairs.

As you reach the top, you are aware of many doors with signs on them... The door that attracts you most is the **Relaxation Room**. So enter into it now and see the beautiful Jacuzzi with the water gently moving. Disrobe now and step into the Jacuzzi, and feel how different this water feels, so silky and soft. As it flows gently over your skin, you feel the relaxing effects on your skin, and you feel your cells being cleansed, and you know now this is not just ordinary water.

This is magical, mystical water... And you feel the water flowing past the surface of the skin and down through the tissues, and muscles and the bones... all of your cells....Now you feel your cells being opened and cleansed of toxins and residue which is unnecessary... Feel your organs being cleansed. Feel the water flowing through every part of your body. Just let go and release those toxins, those poisons, those tensions. Just exhale now and let go... (Pause)

Now relaxed and refreshed, step out of the Jacuzzi and put your clothes back on and exit the relaxation room to the hallway. In the hallway see another room with a sign saying **Media Room.** Enter into this room now and see all of the equipment. All of the equipment that you could possibly want in a mixed media room - computers, books, stereos, CD equipment, paint, easels, drawing pads, pencils, clay – everything that any artist would need to create.

Look around now and add any other equipment that you would like to have... Now sit down in front of a clump of clay, or in front of an easel, or a computer, and create a 3-dimensional **image of you** as you would like to be. Perhaps you would like to be slimmer, or stronger, or more confident.

Create that image now... Make sure you put in every detail... including the expressions on your face... See this completed 3-dimensional you as not only a possibility of what you can become, but this is who you really are underneath the layer of limiting thoughts and emotions which you have stored. (pause)

See yourself in this figure as the real you. Now take that 3-dimensional figure and add more color to the scene...turn up the light and make the image brighter... and make the whole image larger... and as you observe this **"REAL YOU"** – brighter, more colorful – add the emotion of **desire**....

As you see this image, desire this image to be you. Feel that desire in your chest now. Look at the image and feel that desire. You wish to be this image. Feel it... now add a second emotion, the emotion of **belief.** Believe this **IS** really you, right now. Believe it. Feel that in your chest. Feel the belief that this is you... and now a third emotion, add **expectance.** Expect this image to be the real you, right now. Expect it, just as if you were expecting a wonderful gift. For now you realize that this is a gift, and you hold it within you...

Now remember this image and the three emotions of desire, belief and expectancy. And know that **the subconscious does everything in its power to create what it perceives you to be, and right now it perceives you to be** this image... The more you see this image, the more powerful this image has an effect on your subconscious.

The more desire, belief, and expectancy you have, the more power the change will be... Now as you look at this image, say the following statements to yourself: **"I believe in myself." "I believe in myself." "I am capable." "I am capable." "I am lovable.""I am lovable." "I am confident." "I am confident." "I feel good about myself." "I feel good about myself."**

You may come back to this special mansion any time. You may go on to the media room and create other images. This image you see now is the real you, and is manifesting right now. Come back to this room often, and every time you do this exercise, you will go deeper and deeper relaxed....

Slowly now, we're going to come back to this room where you are. As I count from 1 to 5, you'll have a choice of opening your eyes at the number 5, or going on to a deeper state of relaxation and sleep.

1, Feeling better than you have felt in a long time...

2, Believing in how lovable and confident you really are...

3, Start becoming aware of your surroundings...

4, Feel a coolness flowing over your eyes, like they're being bathed by a mountain stream...

5, Eyes open when you're ready, feeling refreshed and relaxed, like you've just had a wonderful massage and shower."

Informative Links on Anger in Children

1. Tips For Anger Management In Children:
   http://www.angermanagementstrategy.com/Anger-Management-In-Children.php
2. Can Anger in Children be a Sign of Something Serious?
   http://www.help-your-child-with-anger.com/anger-in-children.html
3. Article: 7 Ways to Help the Angry Child:
   http://www.askdrsears.com/topics/discipline-behavior/7-ways-help-angry-child
4. Article: Anger Management for Children:
   http://www.angermanagementtips.com/children.html
5. Anger Overload in Children: Diagnostic and Treatment Issues:
   http://www.greatschools.org/parenting/teaching-values/796-anger-overload.gs
6. Articles: Taking Charge of Anger:
   http://kidshealth.org/kid/feeling/emotion/anger.html
7. Article: Children's Anger and Tantrums:
   http://www.ext.colostate.edu/pubs/consumer/10248.html
8. Anger management for Children:
   http://www.scholastic.com/resources/article/anger-management-for-children/

9. How can teens deal with anger?
   http://kidshealth.org/teen/your_mind/emotions/deal_with_anger.html
10. Teenager anger:
    http://psychcentral.com/library/teen_anger.html
11. Teen anger and aggression:
    http://www.teenlinkusa.com/anger.html

Apps for Mental Health

http://www.huffingtonpost.com/2014/10/27/apps-anxiety_n_6054270.html "5 Apps to Help you cope with Anxiety"

https://www.buzzfeed.com/ariannarebolini/amazing-apps-for-anyone-living-with-anxiety?utm_term=.qin1wpVDpO#.rq9726MO6x "14 Amazing Apps for Anyone Living with Anxiety"

https://itunes.apple.com/us/app/self-help-for-anxiety-management/id666767947?mt=8 "Self-Help for Anxiety Management App"

http://www.adaa.org/finding-help/mobile-apps "Mental Health Apps"

http://www.healthline.com/health/anxiety/top-iphone-android-apps#2 "The 15 Best Anxiety iPhone and Android Apps of 2015"

https://www.anxiety.org/4-apps-for-anxiety-and-depression "Reduce anxiety and depression by using these apps."

http://kidsrelaxation.com/uncategorized/7-apps-to-help-kids-relax/ "7 apps to Help Kids Relax"

http://www.adaa.org/finding-help/mobile-apps "Mental Health Apps"

https://play.google.com/store/apps/details?id=com.excelatlife.depression&hl=en "Depression CBT Self-Help Guide."

http://appadvice.com/applists/show/apps-for-depression **"Apps to fight Depression."**

http://www.healthline.com/health/depression/top-iphone-android-apps#2 **"The best depression iphone and android apps of the year."**

http://learningworksforkids.com/2013/08/great-apps-to-help-kids-cope-with-depression/ **"Great apps to help kids cope with depression."**

http://psychcentral.com/blog/archives/2013/09/20/top-10-free-mental-health-apps/ **"Top 10 free mental health apps."**

https://www.anxiety.org/4-apps-for-anxiety-and-depression **"Reduce anxiety and depression by using these apps."**

http://www.thementalhealthblog.com/2014/06/5-best-iphone-apps-for-overcoming-depression/3/ **"5 best iPhone apps for overcoming depression."**

http://appadvice.com/applists/show/apps-for-depression **"Apps to fight depression."**

YouTube Videos

https://www.youtube.com/watch?v=8_jcEpwKQXc "Guided Meditation – Anxiety Relief"

https://www.youtube.com/watch?v=Ybkh4ekVWug "How does EMDR work?"

https://www.youtube.com/watch?v=hhTcVQ3ZaLs "Approaching Depression with EMDR Therapy"

https://www.youtube.com/watch?v=55BLzhHBkVc "EMDR Therapy Session self administered."

https://www.youtube.com/watch?v=OVi7yX9X35A "EMDR for Racing Thoughts."

https://www.youtube.com/watch?v=Tc8cCaLNsqc "Self-Administered EMDR therapy for freedom from Anxiety, Anger, and Depression."

https://www.youtube.com/watch?v=DPHp1ielut0 "EMDR Therapy: Paper-boats Guided Meditation."

https://www.youtube.com/watch?v=AwRLrnlSl78&list=PL526PJmJkdkS5wVkYSLwKxOvjLtYD5m8Y "EMDR – Smile and feel Positive."

https://www.youtube.com/watch?v=v5IRwMqZSMg "EMDR – Be Positive 2"

https://www.youtube.com/watch?v=xb-pke3ud0E "Childhood Trauma and the Process of Healing (by Daniel Mackler)" https://www.youtube.com/watch?v=AwRLrnlSl78&list=PL526PJ mJkdkS5wVkYSLwKx0vjLtYD5m8Y "EMDR – Smile and feel Positive."

http://www.bing.com/videos/search?q=YouTube+Guided+Imag ery+Grief+and+Loss&&view=detail&mid=29AB532EB1EB91C965 7729AB532EB1EB91C96577&FORM=VRDGAR "Reducing Stress"

https://www.youtube.com/watch?v=ArOfvM-fsHc "You're going to be okay: healing from childhood trauma."

https://www.youtube.com/watch?v=m9Pg4K1ZKws "The effect of trauma on the brain and how it affects behaviors | John Rigg | TEDxAugusta"

https://www.youtube.com/watch?v=d_5DU5opOFk "The Science of Anger"

https://www.youtube.com/watch?v=4Eo6zIcEYhk "How to Control Anger – The Shocking Truth behind your Anger."

https://www.youtube.com/watch?v=-HQIg3ZwAs0 "Get to Know your "Inside Out" Emotions: Anger."

https://www.youtube.com/watch?v=bvteZ_bq0nk "How anger goes out of Control."

https://www.youtube.com/watch?v=BsVq5R_F6RA "Anger Management Techniques"

https://www.youtube.com/watch?v=LRkFQ3DN85E "The Angry Birds Movie – Clip: Red's Anger"

https://www.youtube.com/watch?v=QG4Z185MBJE "Anger, Compassion, and What it means to be Strong."

Books and E-Books by RLT Publishing

"Tragedy, Trauma and Loss in Teens and Pre-Teens: A Parent's Guide"

"Overcoming Drug and Alcohol Problems in Teens and Pre-Teens: A Parent's Guide"

"Overcoming ADHD in Teens and Pre-Teens: A Parent's Guide"

"Overcoming Anxiety in Teens and Pre-Teens: A Parent's Guide"

"Overcoming Depression in Teens and Pre-Teens: A Parent's Guide"

Overcoming Obesity in Teens and Pre-Teens: A Parent's Guide"

"Overcoming Self-Esteem Problems in Teens and Pre-Teens: A Parent's Guide"

"Sexual Identity? Moving from Confusion to Clarity"

"Guided Imagery"

"Gay Men's Guide to Love and Relationships"

"Validation Addiction: Please Make Me Feel Worthy"

"Addicted Physicians: Healing the Healer"

"Addicted Nurses: Healing the Caregiver"

"Addicted Pilots: Flight Plan for Recovery"

"Addicted Pharmacists: Healing the 'Medicine Man'"

"The Traveling Parent"

"Tech Etiquette: OMG"

"Winged Lion of Babylon"

"Tragedy, Trauma, and Loss: Healing the Emotional Wounds"

If you feel someone else could benefit by reading this Book, then please go back to Amazon where you purchased it and do a REVIEW.

Thank you......RLT Publishing

An Excerpt from: "Overcoming Drug and Alcohol Problems in Teens and Pre-Teens: A Parent's Guide" by Dr. Richard L. Travis

"Why Some Children Start Using Drugs

There is a strange, and yet very commonplace opinion that only children from poor and needy families are at risk to become drug or alcohol addicted. Unfortunately, this is not true, and alcohol or drug abuse depends on different factors, and social status is not the most important one. One of the main reasons why children start abusing drugs is **the environment**. If your kid's friends have alcohol or drug problems and they hang out with bad or troubled teens – there is a great possibility that your child will start doing the same. Living in a rough neighborhood could also lead to problems with drugs and alcohol as well.

Previous family history of substance usage

 If someone in your family is or was abusing drugs and a child witnessed that process – he will consider it to be normal and will likely start taking drugs as well. Also, countless studies have proven the genetic link in terms of addiction. Teenagers with parents, grandparents or other relatives who had a drinking or drug problem are more likely to develop alcoholism themselves.

Conflict at home

If parents live separately, fight regularly, have recently divorced or do not pay much attention to keeping the family harmonious and together, then their children are influenced by an unhealthy family environment. These children might start abusing drugs and alcohol to self-medicate their pain, while others will do it as an act of rebellion against the parents who are causing them stress."

About the Author

Dr. Richard Travis is a Psychotherapist who is in Private Practice in Fort Lauderdale, Florida. In his psychotherapy practice, he has worked with general issues in the population, such as depression, anxiety, and relationship problems. He has also worked with a great many gay men and the HIV population for over twenty (25) years. His specialty in Addictions has allowed him to see how addictions have complicated and destroyed relationships, ruined people's health, and made chaos of their financial situations.

He received his first Master's Degree at Edinboro University of Pennsylvania in Education. He received his second Master's Degree in Counselor Education at Florida Atlantic University in Boca Raton, Florida. He received his Doctorate in Higher Education/Counseling Psychology at Florida International University in Miami, Florida. He has Specialties in Addictions, including State, National and International certifications. He has worked with several people in the healthcare industry who have been in Addiction Monitoring Programs, and currently facilitates several groups a month with professionals being monitored by state and federal agencies.

Dr. Travis has taught classes with every age level of student in Pennsylvania, Michigan and Florida, including teaching graduate Social Work classes at Florida International University in Miami. He has also published several articles on the website Ezinearticles.com.

Made in the USA
San Bernardino, CA
04 December 2019